For

*To the Jackson Family
and Nick Beilenson*

Copyright © 1992
Peter Pauper Press, Inc.
202 Mamaroneck Avenue
White Plains, New York 10601
All rights reserved
ISBN 0-88088-563-7
Library of Congress No. 91-67639
Printed in Singapore
7   6   5   4

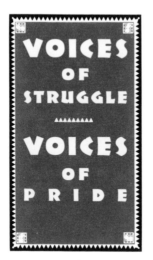

Compiled by
John Beilenson & Heidi Jackson

Design by
Scharr Design

PETER PAUPER PRESS, INC.
WHITE PLAINS · NEW YORK

Introduction

There is a spirit that burns within the African-American community—a strength and pride that four centuries of oppression have been unable to extinguish. *Voices of Struggle, Voices of Pride* is a collection of quotations from some of the African-American men and women whose talent, courage, and determination have led the struggle against racial injustice and for freedom and equality. In generation after generation, this struggle has fueled the African-American spirit.

The political and religious leaders, writers, educators, artists, musicians, and athletes quoted here are also included for their ability to transcend struggle. Flowing from the community's strong identity and undeniable sense of self-worth, these black Americans' lives, words, actions, art, and music—their expressions of pride—have enriched the lives of all Americans.

Unfortunately, this short book cannot include the words of every great African-American. We have attempted to represent a range of perspectives and attitudes within the community, but our work does not pretend to be comprehensive. We would like to include additional voices in a second book of quotations, and encourage you to send your favorites to Peter Pauper Press, 202 Mamaroneck Avenue, White Plains, NY 10601.

For the time being, we hope *Voices of Struggle, Voices of Pride* is educational, inspirational, and enjoyable—a celebration song of the African-American community.

H. J. and J. B.

"I have heard their groans and sighs, and seen their tears, and I would give every drop of blood in my veins to free them."

HARRIET TUBMAN

Voices of Struggle

You have seen how a man was made a slave; you shall see how a slave was made a man.

FREDERICK DOUGLASS

On the 12th of May, 1828, I heard a loud noise in the heavens, and the Spirit instantly appeared to me and said the Serpent was loosened, and Christ had laid down the yoke he had borne for the sins of men, and that I should take it on and fight against the Serpent, for the time was fast approaching when the first should be last and the last should be first. . . . And on the appearance of the sign I should arise and prepare myself, and slay my enemies with their own weapons.

NAT TURNER,
The Confessions of Nat Turner

I would never be any service to anyone as a slave . . .

NAT TURNER,
The Confessions of Nat Turner

There was one of two things I had a *right* to, liberty, or death; if I could not have one, I would have the other; for no man should take me alive; I should fight for my liberty as long as my strength lasted, and when the time came for me to go, the Lord would let them take me.

HARRIET TUBMAN

Strike for your lives and liberties. . . . You cannot be more oppressed than you have been—you cannot suffer greater cruelties than you have already. Rather die freemen than live to be slaves.

HENRY HIGHLAND GARNET

There is a use for almost everything.

DR. GEORGE WASHINGTON CARVER

America owes to my people some of the dividends. . . . She can afford to pay, and she must pay. I shall make them understand that there is a debt to the Negro people which they never can repay. At least, then, they must make amends.

SOJOURNER TRUTH

What, to the American slave, is your Fourth of July? I answer: A day that reveals to him, more than all other days of the year, the gross injustices and cruelty to which he is the constant victim. To him your celebration is a sham.

FREDERICK DOUGLASS

You can't hold a man down without staying down with him.

attributed to BOOKER T. WASHINGTON

The problem of the twentieth century is the problem of the color line.

W. E. B. DU BOIS

No race can prosper till it learns that there is as much dignity in tilling a field as in writing a poem.

BOOKER T. WASHINGTON

If there is anybody in this land who thoroughly believes that the meek shall inherit the earth, they have not often let their presence be known.

W. E. B. DU BOIS

Here I would say that all of my radicalism consists in believing one thing, namely, that all men are created of one blood; that "God created all nations to dwell upon the earth."

B. F. RANDOLPH

Negro action can be decisive. I say that we ourselves have the power to end the terror and to win for ourselves peace and security throughout the land.

PAUL ROBESON

I would crawl on my hands and knees
through mud and mire, to the feet of a
learned man, where I would sit and humbly
supplicate him to instill into me that which
neither devils nor tyrants could remove,
only with my life—for colored people to
acquire learning in this country makes
tyrants quake and tremble on their sandy
foundation.

DAVID WALKER

Speaking like this doesn't mean that we're
anti-white, but it does mean we're anti-
exploitation, we're anti-degradation, we're
anti-oppression.

MALCOLM X

I'm for the Negro. I'm not anti anything.

STOKELY CARMICHAEL

I for one believe that if you give people a
thorough understanding of what confronts
them and the basic causes that produce it,
they'll create their own program, and when
the people create a program, you get action.

MALCOLM X

The adoption of the concept of Black
Power is . . . a call for black people in this
country to unite, to recognize their heritage,
to build a sense of community. . . . It is a
call to reject the racist institutions and
values of this society.

STOKELY CARMICHAEL *and*
CHARLES V. HAMILTON

Non-violence is a powerful and just
weapon. It is a weapon unique in history,
which cuts without wounding and ennobles
the man who wields it. It is a sword that
heals.

MARTIN LUTHER KING, JR.

Divide and conquer, in our world, must become define and empower.

AUDRE LORDE

Revolution is not a one-time event. It is becoming always vigilant for the smallest opportunity to make a genuine change in established, outgrown responses; for instance, it is learning to address each other's difference with respect.

AUDRE LORDE

Revolution accelerates evolution.

KELLY MILLER

You're either part of the solution or part of the problem.

ELDRIDGE CLEAVER

The challenge is to become part of the struggle, to make a positive difference.

DAVID SATCHER

It is time for every one of us to roll up our sleeves and put ourselves at the top of our commitment list.

MARIAN WRIGHT EDELMAN

When it comes to the cause of justice, I take no prisoners and I don't believe in compromising.

MARY FRANCES BERRY

Power never takes a back step—only in the face of more power.

MALCOLM X

I'm not advocating violence. . . . I'm saying I can understand it. If the people are frustrated and feel oppressed and feel this is the only way they can act, I understand. . . . Black America is tired of having their brothers and sisters murdered by the police for no other reason than being black.

SPIKE LEE

"Power concedes
nothing without
a demand.
It never did
and it never will."

FREDERICK DOUGLASS

To protest against injustices is the
foundation of all our American democracy.

THURGOOD MARSHALL

You're not supposed to be so blind with
patriotism that you can't face reality. Wrong
is wrong no matter who does it or says it.

MALCOLM X

The only way to make sure people you
agree with can speak is to support the rights
of people you don't agree with.

ELEANOR HOLMES NORTON

Wars of nations are fought to change maps.
But wars on poverty are fought to map
changes.

MUHAMMAD ALI

He who controls images controls everything.

ROBERT TOWNSEND

The cost of liberty is less than the price of repression.

W. E. B. DU BOIS

If a man hasn't discovered something that he will die for, he isn't fit to live.

MARTIN LUTHER KING, JR.

I'd tell the white powers that I ain't trying to take nothing from them. I'm trying to make Mississippi a better place for all of us. And I'd say, "What you don't understand is that as long as you stand with your feet on my neck, you got to stand in a ditch, too. But if you move, I'm coming out. I want to get us both out of the ditch."

FANNIE LOU HAMER

It is not who you attend school with but
who controls the school you attend.

NIKKI GIOVANNI

The real problem is not the bad guys, it is
that the good guys have gone to sleep.

MAYNARD JACKSON

If we do not now dare everything, the
fulfillment of that prophecy, re-created from
the Bible in song by a slave, is upon us:
*God gave Noah the rainbow sign, No more
water, the fire next time!*

JAMES BALDWIN

It is important not only to have the
awareness and to feel impelled to become
involved, it's important that there be a
forum out there to which one can relate, an
organization, a movement.

ANGELA DAVIS

This constant reminder by society that I am "different" because of the color of my skin, once I step outside of my door, is not my problem—it's theirs. I have never made it my problem and never will. I will die for my right to be human—just human.

CICELY TYSON

The major threat to blacks in America has not been oppression, but rather the loss of hope and absence of meaning.

CORNEL WEST

The American Negro must remake his past in order to make his future. . . .

ARTHUR SCHOMBURG

You cannot fight by being on the outside complaining and whining. You have to get on the inside to be able to assess their strengths and weaknesses and then move in.

SHIRLEY CHISHOLM

The reason Joe Louis will always be respected in the black community is that at a time when other blacks couldn't even talk back to white people, Joe Louis was beating them up, knocking them down and making them bleed.

JESSE JACKSON

If you're going to play the game properly, you'd better know every rule.

BARBARA JORDAN

Intolerance can grow only in the soil of ignorance; from its branches grow all manner of obstacles to human progress.

WALTER WHITE

We should never get too tired or too sophisticated to march. That kind of response never goes out of style.

MARTIN LUTHER KING, SR.

Until relief from oppression is granted, the only appropriate name for America is "you hypocrite!"

DICK GREGORY

We must all learn to live together as Brothers. Or we will all perish together as fools.

MARTIN LUTHER KING, JR.

Black people looked to Washington for fair play and for protection of our civil rights. Instead, we got Pac-Man social policies and cave man civil rights policies.

JOHN E. JACOB,
on the Reagan Administration

If folk can learn to be racist, then they can learn to be antiracist. If being a sexist ain't genetic, then, dad gum, people can learn about gender equality.

JOHNNETTA B. COLE

Sometimes, it's like a hair across your cheek. You can't see it, you can't find it with your fingers, but you keep brushing at it because the feel of it is irritating.

MARIAN ANDERSON,
on racial prejudice

Like an individual who cannot solve a cancer problem, an alcohol problem, or a drug problem by denying it, a nation cannot deal fundamentally with racism by denying its existence. White people don't like to talk about racism because it is ugly.

ROGER WILKINS

All we say is that South Africa preaches what it practices and practices what it preaches; America preaches one thing and practices another.

MALCOLM X

Our dehumanization of the Negro then is indivisible from our dehumanization of ourselves; the loss of our own identity is the price we pay for our annulment of his.

JAMES BALDWIN

Either we must attain freedom for the whole world or there will be no world left for any of us.

WALTER WHITE

We can say "Peace on Earth," we can sing about it, preach about it, or pray about it, but if we have not internalized the mythology to make it happen inside of us, then it will not be.

BETTY SHABAZZ

Much of the anxiety of modern times has been created because white America has been unable and unwilling to recognize Negroes as people on any basis.

LOFTON MITCHELL

"We, the people." It is a very eloquent beginning. But when that document was completed on the seventeenth of September in 1787 I was not included in that "We, the people." I felt somehow for many years that George Washington and Alexander Hamilton just left me out by mistake. But through the process of amendment, interpretation, and court decision I have finally been included in "We, the people."

BARBARA JORDAN

If there is any equality now, it has been our struggle that put it there. Because they said, "All people are created equal." They said "all" and meant "some." They meant "white." All means all, sweetheart.

BEAH RICHARDS

My dad told me way back that you can't use race. For example, there's no difference between a white snake and a black snake. They'll both bite.

THURGOOD MARSHALL

I am an invisible man. . . . I am a man of substance, of flesh and bone, fiber and liquids—and I might even be said to possess a mind. I am invisible, understand, simply because people refuse to see me.

RALPH ELLISON,
The Invisible Man

Racism is a human problem and a crime that is absolutely so ghastly that a person who is fighting racism is well within his rights to fight against it by any means necessary until it is eliminated.

MALCOLM X

You see, black *isn't* beautiful. *White* isn't beautiful. Skin-deep is never beautiful.

JESSE OWENS

Black people are in trouble today. America is in trouble today.

JOHN E. JACOB

It's not because one is black that the prejudice exists. The prejudice exists because one can identify the person who was once a slave or in the lower class, and the caste system can survive longer. In Nazi Germany, they found a way to identify the Jews by putting a label on them to indicate who they were . . . [T]hey needed a mark. But here you have people who are black people.

TONI MORRISON

The common goal of 22 million Afro-Americans is respect as *human beings,* the God-given right to be a *human being.* Our common goal is to retain the *human rights* that America has been denying us. We can never get civil rights in America until our *human rights* are first restored. We will never be recognized as citizens there until we are first recognized as *humans.*

MALCOLM X

"To be born in a free society and not be born free is to be born into a lie."

JAMES BALDWIN

I'd rather see a cat with a processed head
and a natural mind than a natural head and
a processed mind. It ain't what's on your
head, it's what's in it.

H. RAP BROWN

The system conceded to black people the
right to sit up in the front of the bus—a
hollow victory when one's longest trip is
likely to be from the feudal South to the
mechanized poverty of the North.

JULIAN BOND

We must focus on those things within us
that allow others to control us, know those
who would empower themselves to control
us and understand that the forces can be
brown male or female, white male or
female, as well as our selves.

ANDREA CANAAN

To be black and conscious in America is to
be in a constant state of rage.

JAMES BALDWIN

Goddammit, look! We live here and they live there. We black and they white. They got things and we ain't. They do things and we can't. It's just like living in jail.

RICHARD WRIGHT,
Native Son

Injustice anywhere is a threat to justice everywhere.

MARTIN LUTHER KING, JR.

White teenagers are more prone to drug addiction than are Blacks but the media continues to perpetuate the story that crack is black.

ISHMAEL REED

The epidemic of drugs and violence in the black community stems from a calculated attempt by whites to force black self-destruction.

LOUIS FARRAKHAN

My response to racism is anger. I have lived with that anger, ignoring it, feeding upon it, learning to use it before it laid my visions to waste, for most of my life. Once I did it in silence, afraid of the weight. My fear of anger taught me nothing. Your fear of that anger will teach you nothing, also.

AUDRE LORDE

It was a damn fight everywhere I was, every place I worked, in New York, in Hollywood, all over the world.

LENA HORNE

Ever since I've gotten to New York, I've had to hold everything back. I'm playing in a white man's world. I know that. So I've held it back—until now. I've seen things in New York that are 100 times worse than anything I ever saw in the South, in Virginia, where I grew up. New York is a time bomb. I wouldn't want my kids growing up there. If something doesn't happen soon, it's going to be a hellhole.

LAWRENCE TAYLOR

If you're afraid to die, you will not be able
to live.

JAMES BALDWIN

I say violence is necessary. It is as American
as cherry pie.

H. RAP BROWN

In the act of resistance the rudiments of
freedom are already present.

ANGELA DAVIS

I am not tragically colored. There is no
great sorrow dammed up in my soul, nor
lurking behind my eyes. I do not mind at
all. . . . I do not weep at the world—I am
too busy sharpening my oyster knife.

ZORA NEALE HURSTON

The cost of living is going up and the chance of living is going down.

FLIP WILSON

No person is your friend who demands your silence, or denies your right to grow.

ALICE WALKER

Reality has changed chameleonlike before my eyes so many times, that I have learned, or am learning, to trust almost anything except what appears to be so.

MAYA ANGELOU

Negro women, historically, have carried the dual burden of Jim Crow and Jane Crow.

PAULI MURRAY

If you don't know where you come from, it's difficult to assess where you are. It's even more difficult to plan where you are going.

JOSEPH LOWERY

I have a bias which leads me to believe that no problem of human relations is ever insoluble.

RALPH BUNCHE

We've got to have a legacy of leadership. We've got to bring along with us a generation of black women who are going to confront twenty-first-century realities.

JEWELL JACKSON MCCABE

Black women have not historically stood in the pulpit, but that doesn't undermine the fact that they build the churches and maintain the pulpits.

MAYA ANGELOU

They say I'm a witch with a "b" on the front. It's the age-old problem. Someone else would be called a shrewd businessman. Women are called other things.

ANITA BAKER

Black women are not here to compete or fight with you, brothers. If we have hangups about being male or female, we're not going to be able to use our talents to liberate all of our black people.

SHIRLEY CHISHOLM

The grim possibility is that she who "hides her brains" will, more than likely, end up with a mate who is only equal to a woman with "hidden brains" or none at all.

LORRAINE HANSBERRY

I want the same thing for blacks, Hispanics, and whites that I want for myself and my child. And that is the ability to take charge of our lives and not be victimized by reproduction.

FAYE WATTLETON

Feminism is the political theory and practice that struggles to free *all* women: women of color, working-class women, poor women, disabled women, lesbians, old women—as well as white, economically privileged, heterosexual women. Anything less than this vision of total freedom is not feminism, but merely female self-aggrandizement.

BARBARA SMITH

No one can dub you with dignity. That's yours to claim.

ODETTA

It is the easiest thing in the world to say
every broad for herself—saying it and acting
that way is one thing that's kept some of us
behind the eight ball where we've been
living for a hundred years.

BILLIE HOLIDAY

I used to want the words "She tried" on my
tombstone. Now I want "She did it."

KATHERINE DUNHAM

Thoughts have power. Thoughts are
energy. And you can make your world or
break your world by your thinking.

SUSAN L. TAYLOR

If people are informed they will do the right
thing. It's when they are not informed that
they become hostages to prejudice.

CHARLAYNE HUNTER-GAULT

34

I just think there's nothing we can't do. I never considered it to be a disadvantage to be a Black woman. I never wanted to be anything else. We have brains! We're beautiful! We should be able to do anything we set our minds to!

DIANA ROSS

I'm not a feminist. . . . I'm just a proud black woman. I don't need to be labeled.

QUEEN LATIFAH

One of my friends said most people are so hard to please that if they met God, they'd probably say, yes, She's great, but . . .

DIANA ROSS

I think everyone is man and woman. I feel my bothness. I can be optimistic [about relations between the sexes] based on who I am.

ALICE WALKER

"In my life, if you have a purpose in which you can believe, there's no end to the amount of things you can accomplish."

MARIAN ANDERSON

Voices of Pride

We build our temples for tomorrow, strong
as we know how, and we stand on top of
the mountain, free within ourselves.

LANGSTON HUGHES

I have a dream that one day on the red hills
of Georgia the sons of former slaves and the
sons of former slaveowners will be able to
sit down together at the table of
brotherhood.

MARTIN LUTHER KING, JR.

Lift every voice and sing
Till earth and heaven ring
Ring with the harmonies of Liberty
Let our rejoicing rise
High as the glistening skies
Still we'll march on
Till victory is won.

JAMES WELDON JOHNSON

We want to live as free men; not as half
  slaves 'mong the free.
JAMES DAVID CORROTHERS

Men of the Negro race, let me say to you
that a greater future is in store for us; we
have no cause to lose hope, to become faint-
hearted. We must realize that upon
ourselves depend our destiny, our future;
we must carve out that future, that destiny.
MARCUS GARVEY

Black men, you were once great; you shall
be great again. Lose not courage, lose not
faith, go forward.
MARCUS GARVEY

Nothing the future brings can defeat a
people who have come through three
hundred years of slavery and humiliation
and privation with heads high and eyes clear
and straight.
PAUL ROBESON

There is in this world no such force as the force of a man determined to rise. The human soul cannot be permanently chained.

W. E. B. Du Bois

Neither the old-time slavery, nor continued prejudice need extinguish self-respect, crush manly ambition or paralyze effort . . .

Paul Robeson

There is no problem that we can't solve if we can corral our resources behind it. That means people, that means money, that means the good will and cooperation of a large segment of the people.

Coretta Scott King

Freedom is not something that anybody can be given; freedom is something people take and people are as free as they want to be.

James Baldwin

Perhaps we shall be the teachers when it is done. Out of the depths of pain we have thought to be our sole heritage in this world—O, we know about love!

And that is why I say to you that, though it be a thrilling and marvelous thing to be merely young and gifted in such times, it is doubly so, doubly dynamic—to be young, gifted and Black.

LORRAINE HANSBERRY

Never say: "Let well enough alone." . . . Be discontented. Be dissatisfied. "Sweat and grunt" under present conditions. Be as restless as the tempestuous billow on the boundless sea. Let your discontent break mountain-high against the wall of prejudice, and swamp it to the very foundation. Then we shall not have to plead for justice nor on bended knee crave mercy; for we shall be men.

RIDGELY TORRENCE,
The Story of John Hope

Black people have freed themselves from the dead weight of the albatross of blackness that once hung around their neck. They have done it by picking it up in their arms and holding it out with pride for all the world to see. They have done it by embracing it—not in the dark of the moon but in the searing light of the white sun. They have said *Yes* to it and found that the skin that was once seen as symbolizing their shame is in reality their badge of honor.

SHIRLEY CHISHOLM

The very time I thought I was lost, my dungeon shook and my chains fell off.

AFRICAN-AMERICAN FOLK SAYING

One day in this lifetime, we will reach freedom's gate together and pass through to a land where we will all be judged by our fellow beings for the content of our character rather than the color of our skin.

DAVID DINKINS

Given the odds, we weren't supposed to stop being slaves. Given the opposition, we weren't supposed to have an education. Given the history, we weren't supposed to have families. Given the blues, we weren't supposed to have spirit. Given the power of the enemy, we weren't supposed to fight back. Not only have we achieved victories, we have—despite the powers against us—become our own victories.

CAMILLE COSBY

What you don't know, you fear. It is fear that drives us to do many things that we wouldn't otherwise do. But I am a believer. I know He lives and I know He cares for me, and that is a great help with everything.

MARIAN ANDERSON

Lifting as they climb, onward and upward they go struggling and striving and hoping that the buds and blossoms of their desires may burst into glorious fruition ere long.

MARY CHURCH TERRELL

I just want to do God's will. And He's
allowed me to go to the mountains. And
I've looked over, and I've seen the
promised land . . . So I'm happy tonight.
I'm not worried about anything. I'm not
fearing any man.

MARTIN LUTHER KING, JR.

A spiritual renaissance is what is needed
among young African-American people.
Any attempt at building racial and cultural
institutions in our communities without a
spiritual renaissance—a vibrant embrace of
faith—will produce symbols but not
substance.

ANTHONY A. PARKER

Cease to be a drudge, seek to be an artist.

MARY MCLEOD BETHUNE

Inspiration is 95% nature and silence.

ALICE WALKER

You have to know you can win. You have to think you can win. You feel you can win.

SUGAR RAY LEONARD

Never let your head hang down. Never give up and sit down and grieve. Find another way. And don't pray when it rains if you don't pray when the sun shines.

SATCHEL PAIGE

In America, with all of its evils and faults, you can still reach through the forest and see the sun. But we don't know yet whether the sun is rising or setting for our country.

DICK GREGORY

God has been replaced, as he has all over the West, with respectability and air conditioning.

AMIRI BARAKA

"In your lifetime
if you can come
up with one
original idea you
have accomplished
a great deal."

MAX ROACH

The free man is the man with no fears.

DICK GREGORY

My fight is not to be a white man in a black skin, but to inject some black blood, some black intelligence into the pallid main stream of American life, culturally, socially, psychologically, philosophically.

JOHN O. KILLENS

I have a dream that one day this nation will rise up, live out the true meaning of its creed: we hold these truths to be self-evident, that all men are created equal.

MARTIN LUTHER KING, JR.

One of the great measures of a people is its culture, its artistic stature.

PAUL ROBESON

We look too much to museums. The sun
coming up in the morning is enough.

RALPH ELLISON

It is the duty of the younger Negro
artist . . . to change through the force of his
art that old whispering "I want to be
white," hidden in the aspirations of his
people, to "Why should I want to be white?
I am a Negro—and beautiful!"

LANGSTON HUGHES

The process for me that is going to knit up
the culture, knit up the fabric of the family,
the collective family—all of us—one crucial
part of that is that we tell our own stories.
That we learn to tell them and we tell them
in our own words and that they embrace
our values and that we keep on saying
them, in spite of the madness, the chaos
around us, and in spite of the pressure not
to tell it.

JOHN EDGAR WIDEMAN

The landscape should belong to the people
who see it all the time.

AMIRI BARAKA

Man, if you gotta ask you'll never know.
attributed to LOUIS ARMSTRONG,
about jazz

The blues is life. The sun is life. The Black
man is rich with the sun and the Black man
has always been blue. They are equations.
The Black man has soaked up more sun
and blues than anybody else.

WILLIE DIXON

My music calls more for listening, but it'll
still make you shake your head and pat your
feet. If I don't see anybody doing that in
the audience, we ain't getting to them, and
we're playing mostly for spirit, not for
intellect.

DIZZY GILLESPIE

Jazz music is a compelling love affair for the
listener, a risky business for the promoter,
and a way of life for the musician.

PAUL CARTER HARRISON

Music is supposed to wash away the dust of
everyday life.

ART BLAKEY

Rap isn't a black thing. People of all races
need to understand their history and the
history of the other races. If you're white
you need to understand the history of black
people to deal on a respectful basis. And it
works the other way. Black people need to
know that not all white people have money
and that not all white people have it easy.
Hunger, unemployment and illiteracy have
no color. The walls of ignorance which have
been built up need to be torn down.

KRS ONE

It is from the blues that all that may be called American music derives its most distinctive characteristic.

JAMES WELDON JOHNSON

Jazz to me is one of the inherent expressions of Negro life in America: the eternal tom-tom beating in the Negro soul—the tom-tom of revolt against weariness in a white world, a world of subway trains, and work, work, work; the tom-tom of joy and laughter, and pain swallowed in a smile.

LANGSTON HUGHES

I don't know how to sing Black—and I don't know how to sing white, either. I know how to sing. Music is not a color to me. It's an art.

WHITNEY HOUSTON

Jazz is the nobility of the race put into sound; it is the sensuousness of romance in our dialect; it is the picture of the people in all their glory.

WYNTON MARSALIS

I didn't wish for anything I couldn't get, and I got pretty near everything I wanted. They're going to enjoy blowing over me— cats will be coming from everywhere to play. Be good if I get to the Pearly Gates. I'll play a duet with Gabriel. Yeah. We'll play "Sleepy Time Down South."

LOUIS ARMSTRONG

If I hadn't become an entertainer, I would have had to make a noise in some other area. I have always had an enormous need to be seen and heard.

DIAHANN CARROLL

Paris is the dance, and I am the dancer.

JOSEPHINE BAKER

Music is your own experience, your thoughts, your wisdom. If you don't live it, it won't come out of your horn.

CHARLIE PARKER

Acting is just a way of making a living, the family is life.

DENZEL WASHINGTON

Your children need your presence more than your presents.

JESSE JACKSON

A child likes to learn. If children know you want them to do something well, they will always do the best they can.

DOROTHY MAYNOR

"It is impossible to love ourselves without having an affection for Africa."

RANDALL ROBINSON

I suppose too my family directly and my people indirectly have given me the kind of strength that enables me to go anywhere. I can't think where I would be afraid, apprehensive, about going in the world, on this planet. I have had some very rough times in my life . . . so what else is new?

MAYA ANGELOU

Here now in our swiftly paced technological era, it seems to me that not only younger Black people, but we older ones as well, need urgently to show our living grand-parents' generation that we do realize and respect and honor how much we have inherited and benefited because of the experiences which they survived.

ALEX HALEY

My primary concern is with children and families. There's been quite a breakdown in the family in recent years, and I'd love to see families come back into their own.

JOYCE DINKINS

Our society allows people to be absolutely neurotic and totally out of touch with their feelings and everyone else's feelings, and yet be very respectable.

NTOZAKE SHANGE

The ultimate measure of a man is not where he stands in moments of comfort and convenience, but where he stands at times of challenge and controversy.

MARTIN LUTHER KING, JR.

There ain't no man can avoid being born average. But there ain't no reason a man got to be common.

SATCHEL PAIGE

I always wanted to be somebody. If I made it, it's half because I was game enough to take a lot of punishment along the way and half because there were a lot of people who cared enough to help me.

ALTHEA GIBSON

We have produced a world of contented
bodies and discontented minds.

ADAM CLAYTON POWELL

To be left alone on the tightrope of youthful
unknowing is to experience full freedom
and the threat of eternal indecision. Few, if
any, survive their teens. Most surrender to
the vague but murderous pressure of adult
conformity. It becomes easier to die and
avoid conflicts than to maintain a constant
battle with the superior forces of maturity.

MAYA ANGELOU

My fight was against the barriers that kept
Negroes out of baseball. This was the area
where I found imperfection, and where I
was able to fight. And I fought because I
knew it was not doomed to be a losing fight.

JACKIE ROBINSON

Decide on a goal, where you want to go. Be committed and dedicated to that goal. Realize that there will be sacrifices and hurdles to overcome, but you can accomplish what you set out to do.

WARREN MOON

Fear of losing is what makes competitors so great. Show me a gracious loser and I'll show you a perennial loser.

O. J. SIMPSON

I plan on going on living for a long time. You don't have to run from me. You can give me my hugs, my high fives, my kisses.

MAGIC JOHNSON

Every small, positive change we can make in ourselves repays us in confidence in the future.

ALICE WALKER

Great art can only be created out of love. To write in this age is a positive act.

JAMES BALDWIN

I continue to create because writing is a labor of love and also an act of defiance, a way to light a candle in a gale wind.

ALICE CHILDRESS

Poetry is not only dream and vision; it is the skeleton architecture of our lives. It lays the foundations for a future of change, a bridge across our fears of what has never been before.

AUDRE LORDE

Don't hate, it's too big a burden to bear.

MARTIN LUTHER KING, SR.

Real knowledge, properly used, will help anyone.

ROMARE BEARDEN

In complete darkness we are all the same, it is only our knowledge and wisdom that separate us. Don't let your eyes deceive you.

JANET JACKSON

Love is man's natural endowment, but he doesn't know how to use it. He refuses to recognize the power of love because of his love of power.

DICK GREGORY

Knowledge is the prime need of the hour.

MARY MCLEOD BETHUNE

When we view liberation as a scarce resource, something only a precious few of us can have, we stifle our potential, our creativity, our genius for living, learning and growing.

ANDREA CANAAN

You can map out a fight plan or a life plan, but when the action starts it may not go the way you planned, and you're down to your reflexes—which means your training. That's where your roadwork shows. If you cheated on that in the dark of the mornin', well, you're gettin' found out now under the bright lights.

JOE FRAZIER

Love is based on emotion and respect is based on justice.

DICK GREGORY

I'm in the best field to do what I need to do. If you shoot for the stars, and hit the moon, it's okay. But, you've got to shoot for something.

ROBERT TOWNSEND

I try to tell them that the most wonderful thing in the world is to be who you are. That to be Black is to shine and aim high.

LEONTYNE PRICE

I've lived here for 40 years, and even though my circumstances would perhaps allow me to live in a penthouse downtown, I wouldn't trade 135th Street for it. There's a warmth about Harlem. The people of Harlem came to me [as clients] when I was a young lawyer. This is where my business is. I belong here.

PERCY SUTTON

I know who I am and I know who I
bottom-line for: Black folks. With time,
people will appreciate that's where my head
and heart are.

SHARON PRATT DIXON

We cannot afford to settle for being just
average; we must learn as much as we can
to be the best that we can. The key word is
education—that's knowledge—education with
maximum effort.

BILL COSBY

With no sense of history, you exist in a
vacuum. How can you appreciate Mike
Tyson without understanding the significance
of Joe Louis? How can you applaud
Michael Jackson and not realize he stands
on the shoulders of Sammy Davis, Jr.?
Could there be a David Dinkins without an
Adam Clayton Powell?

JESSE JACKSON

In my music, my plays, my films I want to
carry always this central idea: to be African.
Multitudes of men have died for less
worthy ideals; it is even more eminently
worth living for.

PAUL ROBESON

The drums of Africa still beat in my heart.
They will not let me rest as long as there is
a single Negro boy or girl without a chance
to prove his worth.

MARY McLEOD BETHUNE

I must see [Africa], get close to it, because I
can never lose the sense of being a
displaced person here in America because
of my color.

PAULE MARSHALL

Molded on Africa's anvil, tempered down
home.

JULIAN BOND